Also by Sara Goldenthal

Tucker the Spirit Cat

No More Scaredy Cat

For my friend Patches.

Table of Contents

<u>Henri Matisse</u>

<u>Ralph Waldo Emerson</u>

Flowers...

I see them dancing, singing, in families, as parents with babies. They are all individuals, with personal lives, going about their day.

Complete projection? Who knows?

With quantum science being understood the way it is, the nature of "reality" is somewhat up for debate these days. Who's to say the flowers aren't talking to each other, playing laughing, sleeping, and being in love? This is what I see when I look at flowers.

I like to peer down, and get up close and escape into what I imagine is a secret special world, where the flowers rule this world and where everything is filled with magnificent color, movement, texture, and beauty. Whether flowers are sentient beings or not, one thing is certain: they are absolutely beautiful.

I hope that the images to follow - along with the words of some of our most beloved writers, artists and philosophers - takes you on a little magical journey. If that journey is 5 minutes, or 1 hour, or even longer, I hope it brings you a sense of delight and wonder.

Kakuzō Okakura

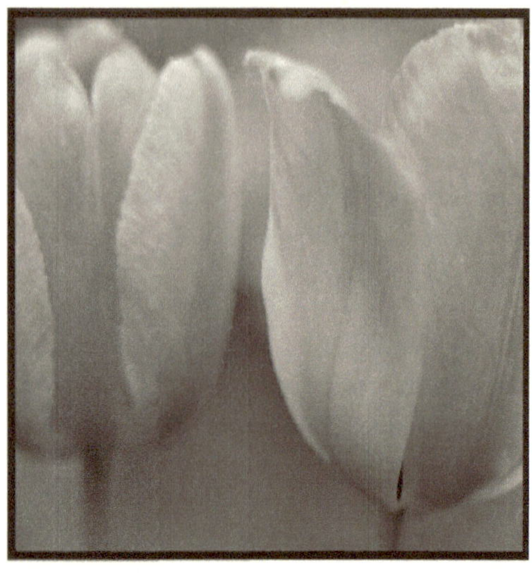

"In joy or sadness flowers are our constant friends."

- The Book of Tea

Claude Monet

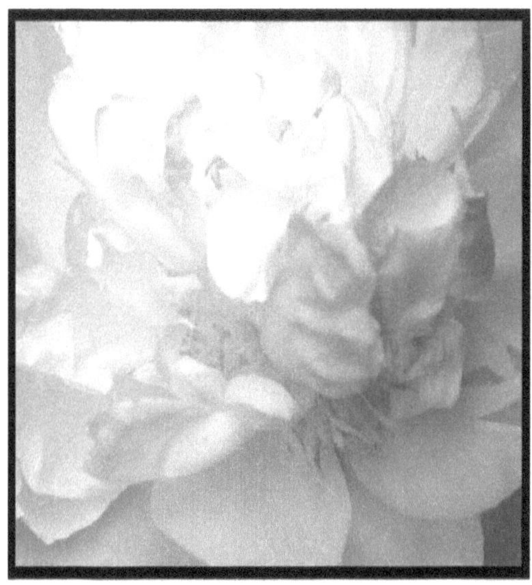

"I must have flowers, always, and always."

Auguste Rodin

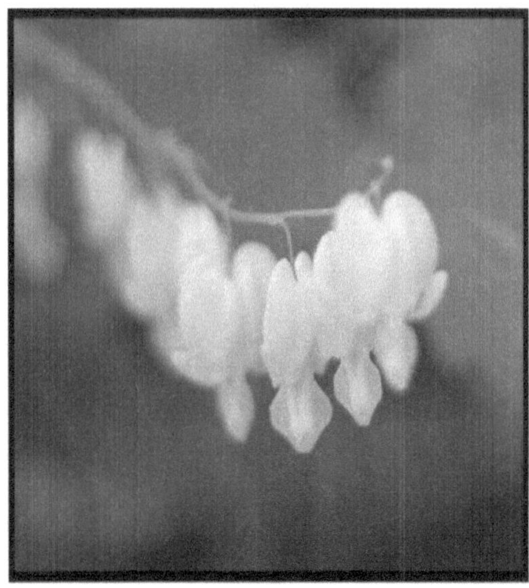

"The artist is the confidant of nature, flowers carry on dialogues with him through the graceful bending of their stems and the harmoniously tinted nuances of their blossoms. Every flower has a cordial word which nature directs towards him."

William Wordsworth

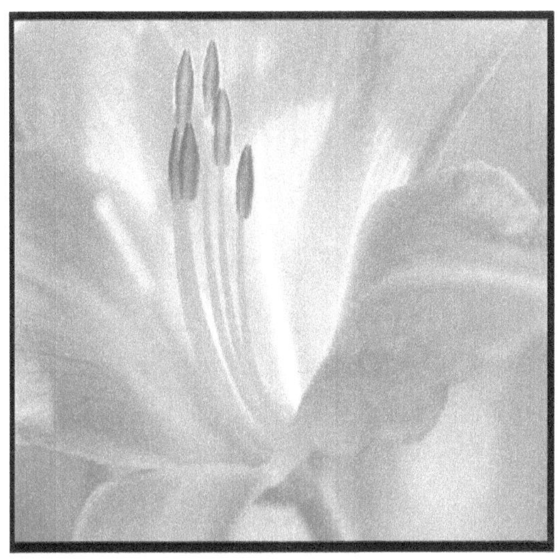

"Tis my faith that every flower
Enjoys the air it breathes!"

- *Lines Written in Early Spring*

Rumi

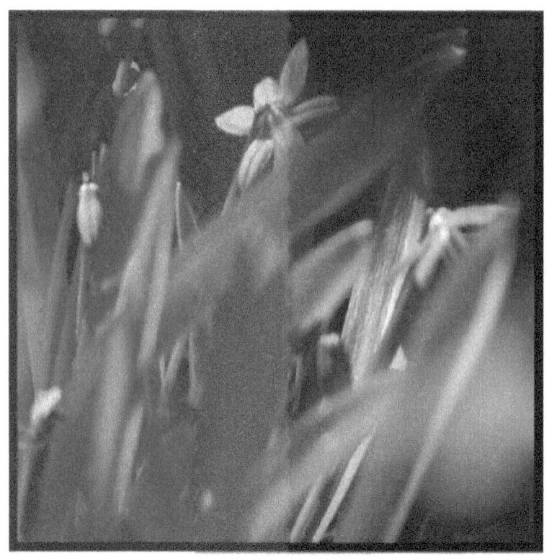

"The flowers will bloom forever,
The birds will sing their eternal song,
The moment we enter the garden,
you and I."

Ikkyu Sojun

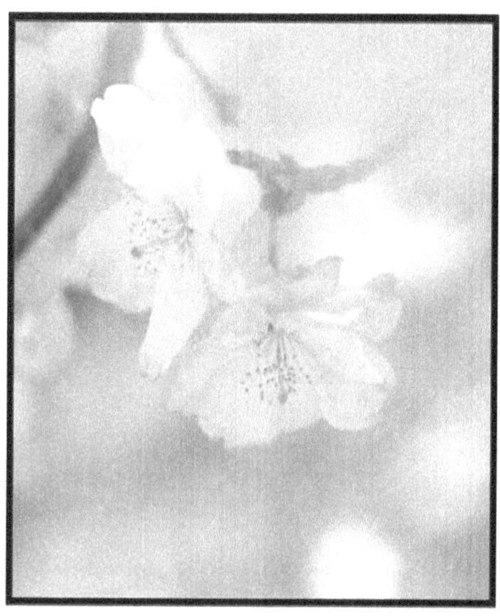

"Break open a cherry tree and there are no flowers, but the spring breeze brings forth myriad blossoms."

Gerard de Nerval

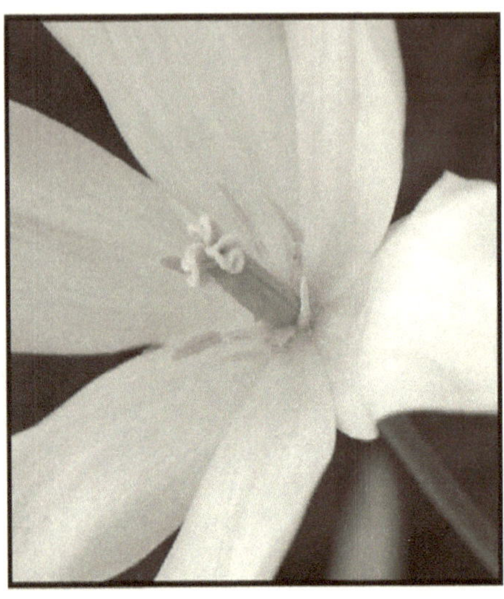

"Every flower is a soul blossoming in nature."

Edward Payson Rod

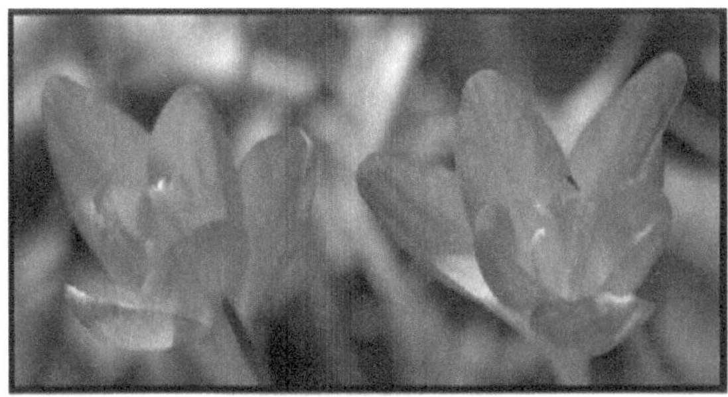

"Look at us, said the violets blooming at her feet, all last winter we slept in the seeming death but at the right time God awakened us, and here we are to comfort you."

Francis Thompson

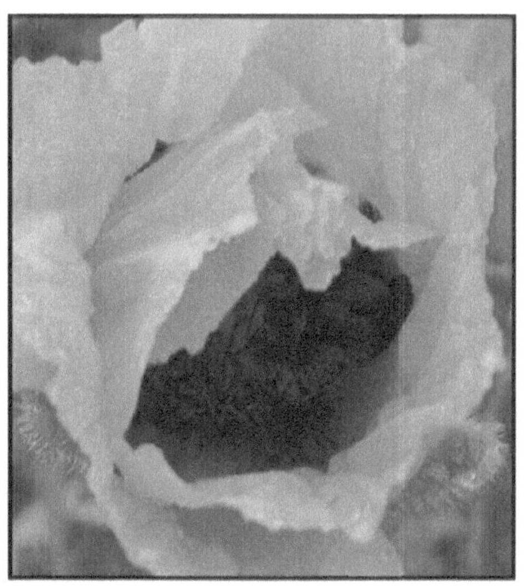

*"Summer set lip to earth's bosom bare,
And left the flushed print in a poppy there."*

*- **The Poppy***

Oscar Wilde

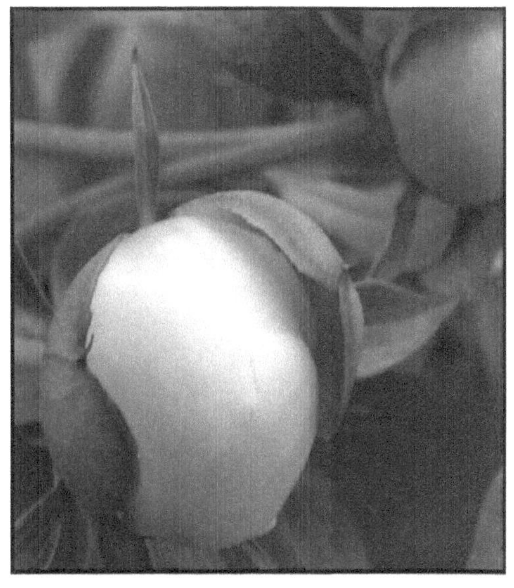

"A flower blossoms for its own joy."

Basho

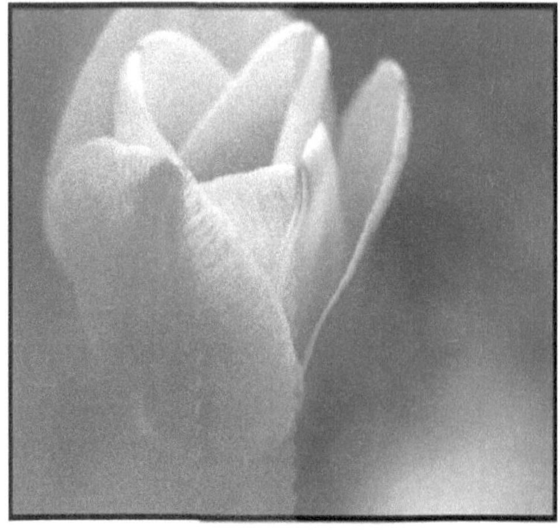

"The temple bell stops but I still hear the sound coming out of the flowers."

Claude Monet

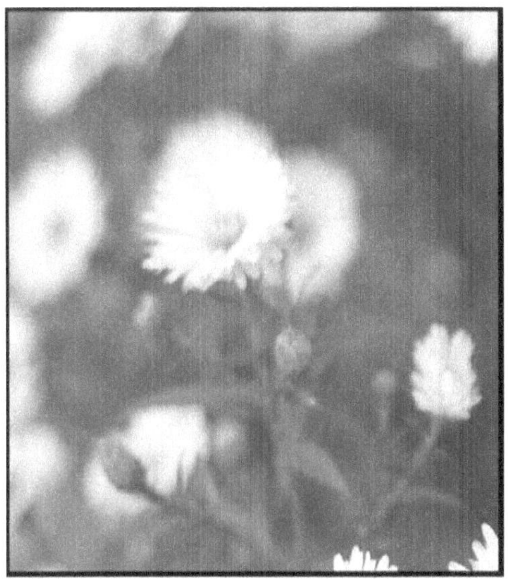

"I perhaps owe having become a painter to flowers."

Chinese Proverb

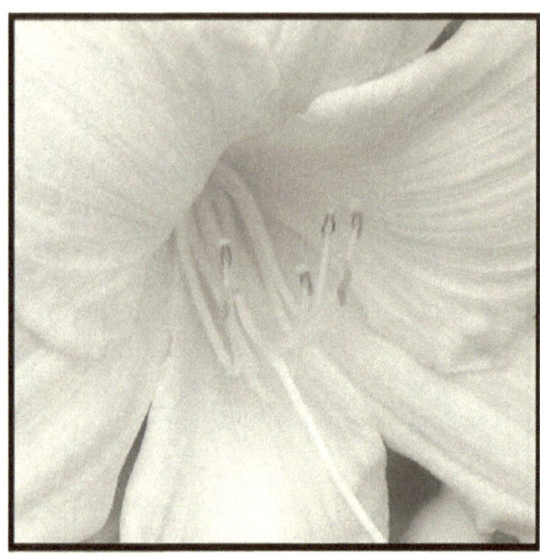

"When you have only two pennies left in the world, buy a loaf of bread with one, and a lily with the other."

Colette

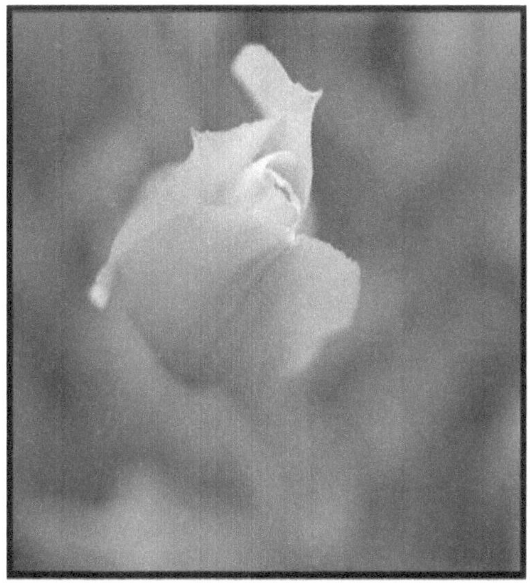

"How can one help shivering with delight when one's hot fingers close around the stem of a live flower, cool from the shade and stiff with newborn vigor!"

L.M. Montgomery

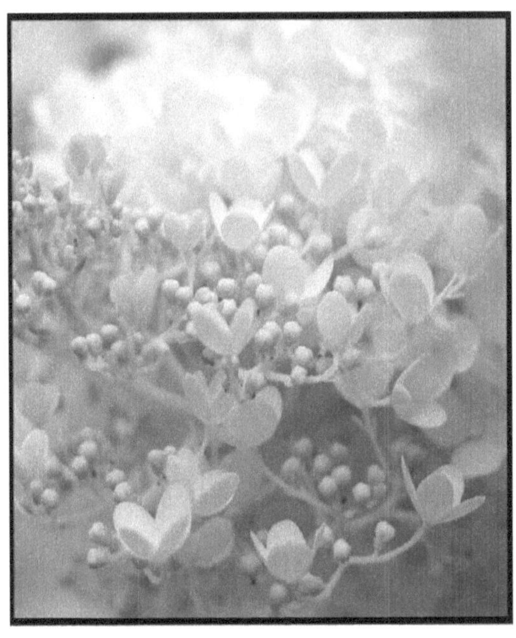

"When weeds go to heaven I suppose they will be flowers."

\-   ***The Story Girl***

The Koran

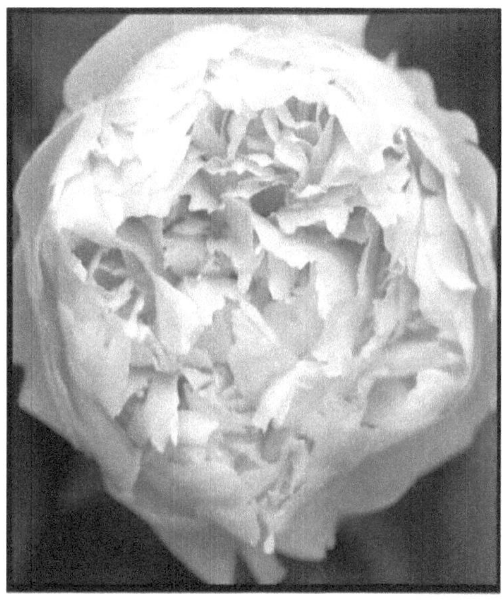

"Bread feeds the body, indeed, but flowers feed also the soul."

William Allingham

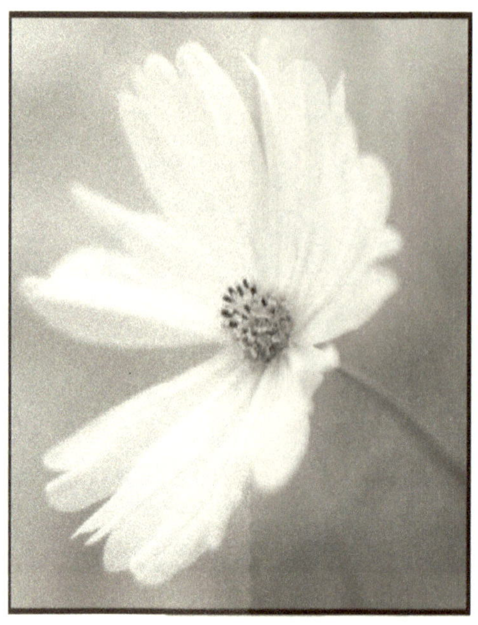

> *"Pluck not the wayside flower;*
> *It is the traveler's dower."*

Gertrude S. Wister

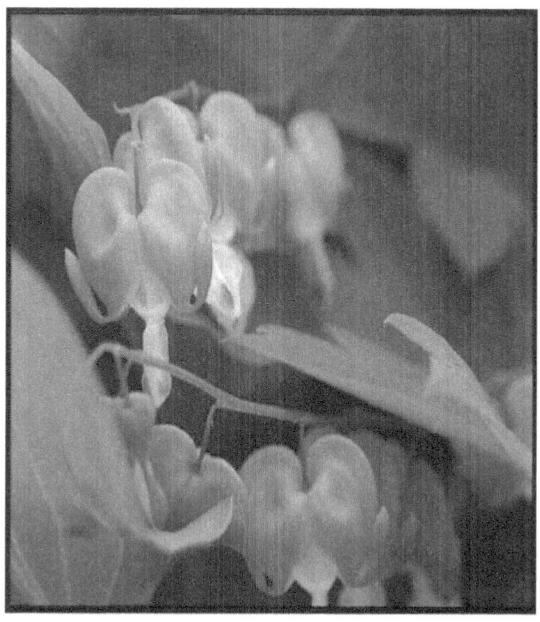

"The flowers of late winter and early spring occupy places in our hearts well out of proportion to their size."

Sir Arthur Conan Doyle

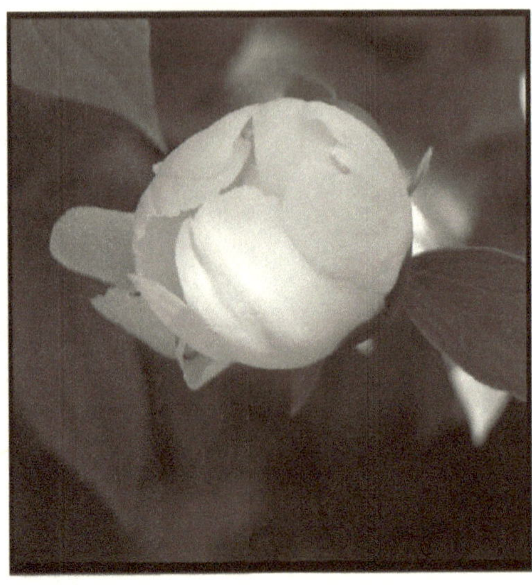

"It is only goodness which gives extras, and so I say again that we have much to hope from the flowers."

Heinrich Heine

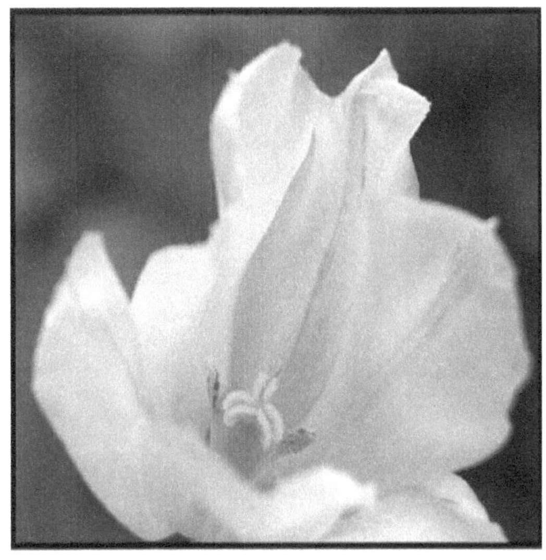

"Perfumes are the feelings of flowers."

Ella Wheeler Wilcox

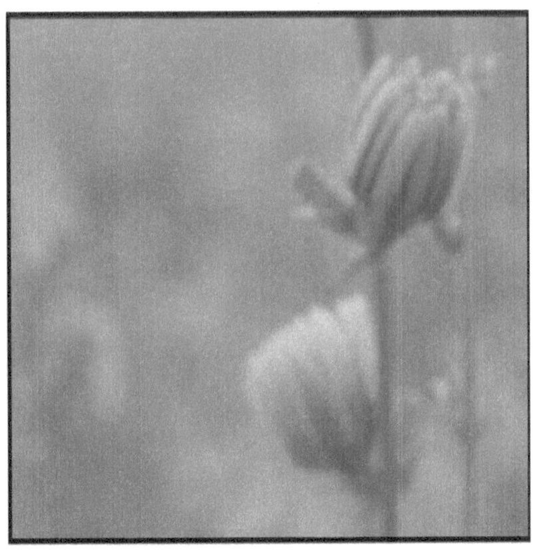

"A weed is but an unloved flower."

Walt Whitman

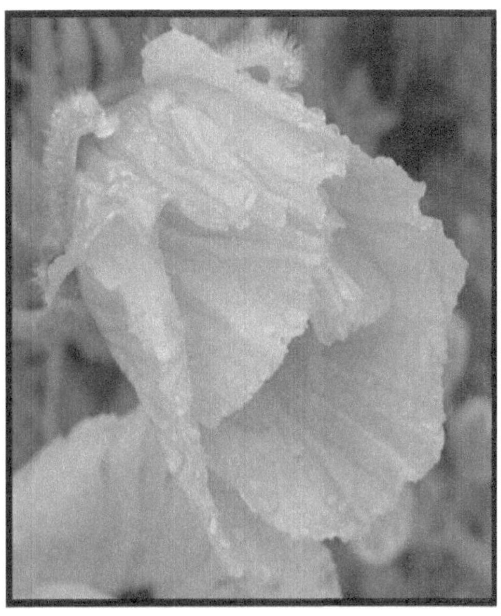

"Give me odorous at sunrise a garden of beautiful flowers where I can walk undisturbed."

Lydia M. Child

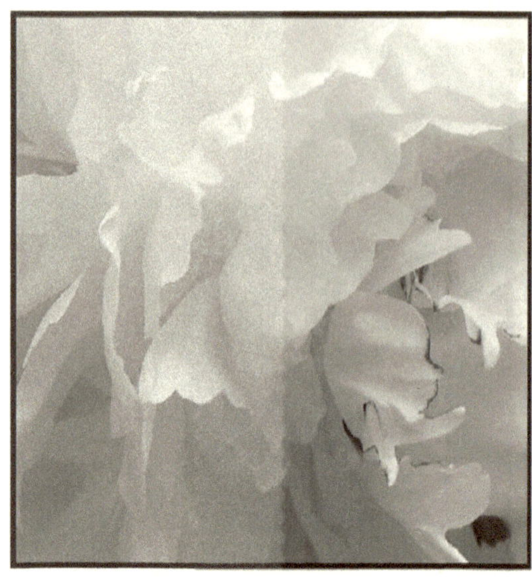

"Flowers have spoken to me more than I can tell in written words. They are the hieroglyphics of angels, loved by all men for the beauty of their character, though few can decipher even fragments of their meaning."

William Wordsworth

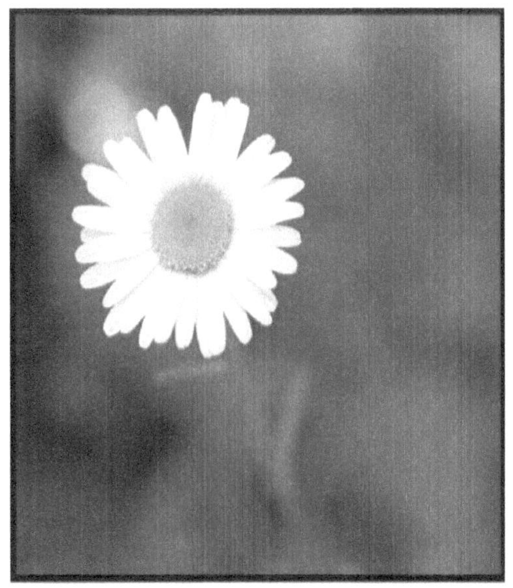

"Thou liv'st with less ambitious aim,
Yet hast not gone without thy fame;
Thou art indeed by many a claim
The Poet's darling."

- **To the Daisy**

Henri Matisse

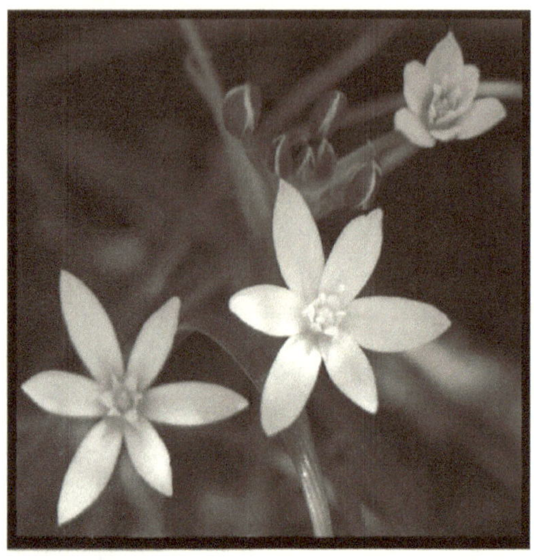

"There are always flowers for those who want to see."

Ralph Waldo Emerson

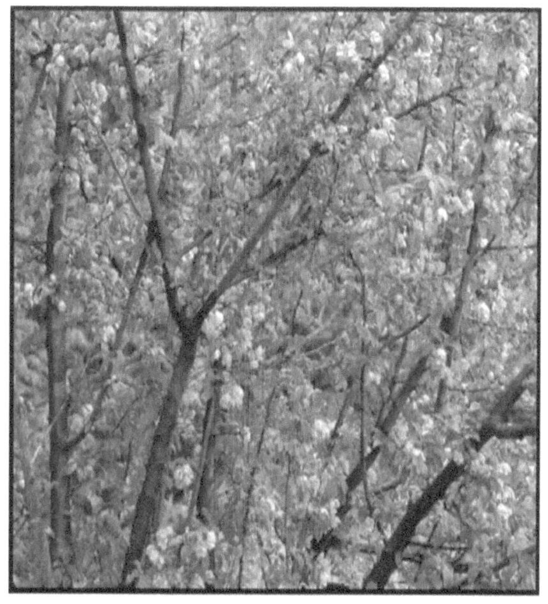

"The earth laughs in flowers."

- *Hamatreya*